Little Books of Guidance

Finding answers to life's big questions!

Also in the series:

T0125883

THE WAY OF LOVE

Go

A little book of guidance

CHURCH
PUBLISHING
INCORPORATED

This book compiles text from the following sources:
Sabrina Alkire and Edmund Newell, *What Can One Person Do? Faith to Heal a Broken World* (New York: Church Publishing, 2005); C. Andrew Doyle, *Unabashedly Episcopalian: Proclaiming the Good News of the Episcopal Church* (New York: Morehouse, 2012); Jenifer Gamber and Bill Lewellis, *Your Faith, Your Life: An Invitation to the Episcopal Church* (New York: Church Publishing, 2017); and Demi Prentiss and Fletcher Lowe, *Radical Sending: Go to Love and Serve* (New York: Morehouse, 2015).

Church Publishing
19 East 34th Street
New York, NY 10016
www.churchpublishing.org

Cover design by Jennifer Kopec, 2Pug Design
Typeset by Denise Hoff

A record of this book is available from the Library of Congress.

ISBN-13: 978-1-64065-178-4 (pbk.)
ISBN-13: 978-1-64065-179-1 (ebook)

Contents

Introduction

I pray that you, being rooted and established in love, may have power, together with all the Lord's holy people, to grasp how wide and long and high and deep is the love of Christ, and to know this love that surpasses knowledge—that you may be filled to the measure of all the fullness of God.

—Ephesians 3:17–19, NIV

At the 79th General Convention of the Episcopal Church in July 2018, Presiding Bishop Michael B. Curry called the Church to practice *The Way of Love*. This is an invitation to all of us, young and old alike, to "grow more deeply with Jesus Christ at the center of our lives, so we can bear witness to his way of love in and for the world."

With this call, Bishop Curry named seven practices that can help us grow deeper in our relationship with God, Jesus, and our neighbors as we also learn how to live into our baptismal promises more fully. In today's world of busy schedules, hurried meals, and twenty-four-hour news cycles, it is now more imperative that we make and take the time to center ourselves and follow the way of Jesus. This might mean revisioning and reshaping the pattern and rhythm of our daily life—finding a slice of time to center our thoughts on Jesus. Within these pages you will find ideas to engage in the practice of go as you walk on *The Way of Love: Practices for a Jesus-Centered Life*.

To be a Christian is to be a seeker. We seek love: to know God's love, to love, and to be loved by others. It also means learning to love ourselves as a child of God. We seek freedom from the many forces that pull us from living as God created us to be: sin, fear, oppression, and division. God desires us to be dignified, whole, and free. We also seek abundant life. This is a life that is overflowing with joy, peace, generosity, and delight. It is a life where there is enough for all because we share with abandon. We seek a life of meaning, giving back to God and living for others and not just for ourselves. Ultimately we seek Jesus. Jesus is the way of love and that has the power to change lives and change the world.

How are we called to practice the Way of Love? Bishop Curry has named seven practices to follow. Like a "Rule of Life" practiced by Christians for almost two thousand years, these are ways that help us live intentionally in our daily life, following our deepest values. These are not add-ons to our day, but ways to recognize God working in us and through us.

Just as Jesus went to the highways and byways, he sends us beyond our circles and comfort, to witness to the love, justice, and truth of God with our lips and with our lives. We go to listen with humility and to join God in healing a hurting world. We go to become Beloved Community, a people reconciled in love with God and one another. We seek and serve Christ in all persons, loving our neighbors as ourselves. We strive for justice and peace among all people and respect the dignity of every human being. With God's help we cross boundaries, listen deeply, and live like Jesus.

Practices are challenging and can be difficult to sustain. Even though we might practice "solo" (e.g., prayer), each practice belongs to the community as a whole in which you inhabit as a whole—your family, church, or group of friends. Join with some trustworthy companions with whom to grow into this way of life; sharing and accountability help keep us grounded and steady in our practices.

This series of seven Little Books of Guidance is designed for you to discover how following certain practices can help you follow Jesus more fully in your daily life. You may already keep a spiritual discipline of praying at meals or before bed, regularly reading from the Bible, or engaging in acts of kindness toward others. If so, build upon what we offer here; if not, we offer a way to begin. Select one of the practices that interests you or that is especially important for you at this time. Watch for signs in your daily life pointing you toward a particular practice. Listen for a call from God telling you how to move closer. Anywhere is a good place to start. This is your invitation to commit to the practices of **Turn—Learn—Pray—Worship—Bless—Go—Rest**. There is no rush, each day is a new beginning. Follow Bishop Curry's call to grow in faith "following the loving, liberating, life-giving way of Jesus. His way has the power to change each of our lives and to change this world."

1 ▪ What Does It Mean to Go?

In the opening chapter of Genesis we learn that God is the God of all creation. Out of God's love, God brought everything into being, the heavens, the earth, all living creatures including humanity, and "it was good." At the very start of the biblical story we learn that God is a God of the whole cosmos, a universal God, who watches over and cares for all of creation. The story continues, however. No sooner had this universal, loving God created humankind than we turned our backs on God. We chose to live unto ourselves. We became alienated from the love and power of God, and we became alienated from each other, and our relationships became distorted. Sin is less about actions and more about a state of separation, separation from God, separation from each other, separation from all creation. Sin is about isolation, division, and broken relationships.

But God does not want humans to be alienated from God and from each other. The loving Creator chooses to rebuild the bonds of love that are severed through human sin. God's mission is to reconnect with humanity and heal the divisions that separate us. The central element of God's mission, the *missio Dei,* is God's commitment to restore to unity that which had become broken, to reconcile a divided world, to heal a hurting humanity.

To fulfill this mission God chose a particular people as an entry point into the world. Through Abraham and Sarah and their descendants, God began a new relationship with humankind. God says to Abraham:

> Behold, my covenant is with you, . . . and you shall be the
> father of a multitude of nations. . . . I will make you

1

exceedingly fruitful; and I will make nations of you, and kings shall come forth from you. And I will establish my covenant between me and you and your descendants after you throughout their generations for an everlasting covenant, to be God to you and to your descendants after you. And I will give to you, and to your descendants after you, the land of your sojournings, all the land of Canaan, for an everlasting possession; and I will be their God. (Genesis 17:2–8)

The whole of Hebrew scripture is the telling and retelling of the quest for relationship between God and God's chosen people.

To help define this relationship God gave the Law. The Law stood as God's assurance of God's love and faithfulness. In Exodus God promises Moses and his people:

If you will obey my voice and keep my covenant, you shall be my own possession among all peoples; for all the earth is mine, and you shall be to me a kingdom of priests and a holy nation. (Exodus 19:5–6)

The Law stood as God's assurance of love and faithfulness. In the giving of the Law, God sought to establish Israel as the leadership of a new world order. By following God's commandments, the chosen people would stand as a beacon of hope in a world separated from God.

God's covenant with the Jews was not, however, an exclusive arrangement. The new relationship begun with Abraham, and clarified by the Law, was intended for all of humanity. God's covenant was to be the vehicle, the door, by which all the peoples of the world could be joined both to the almighty Creator and to each other. Israel was to serve as a centripetal force pulling all of humanity back into relationship with God.[1]

Abraham and Sarah's descendants thus were to be agents of reconciliation between God and an errant humanity. All the nations were to come to God through the covenant. The prophets, especially the servant songs of Isaiah, testify to this calling. In Isaiah 42 God says to God's chosen people:

> I am the Lord, I have called you in righteousness, I have taken you by the hand and kept you; I have given you as a covenant to the people, a light to the nations, to open the eyes that are blind, to bring out the prisoners from the dungeon, from the prison those who sit in darkness. (Isaiah 42:6–7)

And again in Isaiah 49:

> "It is too light a thing that you should be my servant to raise up the tribes of Jacob and to restore the survivors of Israel; I will give you as a light to the nations, that my salvation may reach to the end of the earth." (Isaiah 49:6)

The servant songs of Isaiah proclaim clearly that God's mission in the world is to bring salvation to the ends of the earth; to set free those who are oppressed; to open the eyes of the blind (Isaiah 42:6–7); to heal the separation between God, humanity, and all of creation; to restore to unity with God all the peoples of the world and all of creation. In Isaiah we find the affirmation of Israel's commission, or co-mission, with God.

The story of God's mission, however, does not end with Abraham's covenant. It goes on. As Christians we affirm that because of God's love for the world and desire to be united with all of humanity, God took one final decisive step. In the incarnation of Jesus Christ, God enters the world anew and takes the responsibility for God's mission directly upon himself:

> "For God so loved the world that he gave his only Son, that whoever believes in him should not perish but have eternal life. God sent the Son into the world not to condemn the world, but that the world might be saved through him." (John 3:16–17)

In Jesus, God creates a new covenant, a new means by which all the world could be joined to the Creator. Jesus was sent into the world to be the way, the truth, and the life (John 14:6). As the human form of the creator God, Jesus's mission is coterminous, one and the same, with that of the Creator. His mission is God's mission.

The ultimate act of Jesus's self-giving participation in God's mission is his sacrifice upon the cross and victory over death. The joining of Jesus's pain and suffering on the cross with our pain and suffering where we are passionately connected with God, with one another, and with all creation. On the cross is where this new relationship, this right relationship, with God and each other is effected. In Jesus's resurrection we are given the promise of restored life in him. This is what we mean by Jesus's atonement: his atonement is our at-one-ment, our at-one-ment with God and our at-one-ment with each other. In Jesus's death and resurrection we are given the means by which we become one with each other and with God. In the death and resurrection of Jesus, the divisions between God and humanity are overcome, and the promise of reconciliation is made real.

The reality that Jesus takes on God's mission in his incarnation, death, and resurrection is not a departure from the mission that God entrusted to Israel. Jesus did not come to break down the Law but to fulfill it. Jesus testifies to his fulfillment of the Isaiah prophesy in Luke's Gospel:

> "The Spirit of the Lord is upon me, because he has anointed me to preach good news to the poor. He has sent me to proclaim release to the captives and recovering of sight to the blind, to set at liberty those who are oppressed, to proclaim the acceptable year of the Lord." (Luke 4:18–19)

Over and over again, Jesus demonstrates his solidarity with, and preferential option for, the poor, the sick, the outcasts, and those at the periphery of society. The Gospels are a living testimony to Jesus's life and ministry as the source of God's salvation for the world. In Jesus the reign of God is made real and tangible in our broken world.

Although Jesus is the fulfillment of the Law and prophets, there is, however, a difference between God's mission as it was entrusted to the Jews and how it was realized in Jesus the Christ. Whereas Israel represented a calling-in of humanity to union with God, Jesus turned the direction of God's mission around. Instead of a centripetal force, God's mission, realized in Jesus and empowered by the Holy Spirit, becomes a centrifugal force, a going out. Jesus demonstrates in word and deed that the reign of God, made real in the sending of God's Son, must continue to expand, to move out to the ends of the earth. "As you have sent me into the world, so I have sent them into the world" (John 17:18). Jesus thus sends out his disciples, empowered by the Holy Spirit, to be the bearers of his mission, God's mission, in the world.

> And Jesus called to him the twelve and began to send them out two by two and gave them authority over unclean spirits. . . . So they went out and preached that people should repent. And they cast out many demons, and anointed with oil many that were sick and healed them. (Mark 6:7, 12–13)

And to the seventy Jesus said:

> "Go your way; Whenever you enter a town and they receive you, eat what is set before you; heal the sick in it and say to them, 'The Kingdom of God has come near to you.'" (Luke 10:3, 8–9)

Notice here that God's mission, fulfilled in the incarnation of Jesus and then furthered by the sending-out of the disciples in the power of the Spirit, is multiform. There is loving service, feeding the hungry, healing the sick, and setting free the oppressed. But these acts of love are always coupled with the proclamation of the kingdom of heaven. In other words, God's mission to unite all of humanity to one another and to God is realized through acts of love and justice combined with the proclamation of Jesus as the Christ, the Savior of the world. The wholeness of God's mission is discovered in the combination of Jesus's "new commandment"—"Just as I have loved you, you also should love one another (John 13:34)—with the Great Commission, to make disciples of all nations, baptizing them in the name of the Father and the Son and the Holy Spirit (Matthew 28:19).

The movement of God's mission in heralding and making real the reign of God to the ends of the earth is exemplified in the life and writings of Paul. We cannot develop here the complete mission theology of Paul, but we do want to highlight two fundamental aspects of Paul's own role in God's mission. The first is that Paul and his coworkers reached out to the Gentiles with the good news of Jesus Christ. It is true that in the Gospels we are given evidence of Jesus's mission to the Gentiles: see, for example, our Lord's healing of the centurion's slave (Luke 7:1–10) and his curing of the Canaanite woman's daughter (Matthew 15:21–28). But it is in the life and ministry of Paul that God's mission expands beyond Palestine. The second thing we want to emphasize about Paul's mission theology is the full development of the church as the body of Christ in the world today. In the Letter to the Ephesians (probably written by one of Paul's disciples) we find testimony that all who follow Jesus Christ, Jew and Gentile alike, are united with God the Creator:

> And Jesus came and preached peace to you who were far off and peace to those who were near; for through him we both have access in one Spirit to the Father. So then you are no longer strangers and sojourners, but you are fellow citizens with the saints and members of the household of God, built upon the foundation of the apostles and prophets, Christ Jesus himself being the cornerstone, in whom the whole structure is joined together and grows into a holy temple of the Lord; in whom you also are built into it for a dwelling place of God in the Spirit. (Ephesians 2:17–22)

As followers of Jesus Christ today, as the church, we too share in this household of God and thus are called to preach peace to those who are far off and to those who are near. Participation in God's mission, therefore, is at the heart of the baptismal call. Baptism is our commission, co-mission, in God's mission. In the "catechism" in the Book of Common Prayer, we find a profound missiological affirmation of the relationship between the church and God's mission. This catechism states, "The mission of the Church is to restore all people to unity with God and each other in Christ."[2] The calling of the church, the calling of every Christian of any denomination, is to participate with God in the restoration of unity between ourselves and God and ourselves and each other—to participate in the *missio Dei*. It is the work of the church to herald and effect the new order where alienation, division, and separation give way to inclusion, reconciliation, and unity. As the body of Christ in the world today, we are called to work for the restoration to unity of all people with God and each other in Christ. The eminent missiologist David Bosch has summarized it thus:

> Mission is, primarily and ultimately, the work of the Triune God, Creator, Redeemer, and Sanctifier, for the sake of the world, a ministry in which the church is privileged to participate. This is the deepest source of mission. . . . There is mission because God loves people.[3]

Our identity as followers of Christ is dependent upon, and judged against, how faithful we are to the mission of God, to the making real of God's reconciling love in the world. As Christians, we are called to live beyond ourselves, trusting that God will use us to effect

God's restoration to unity—God's redemption of creation to wholeness and oneness in Christ.

Our Call to Go on God's Mission

The church as the body of Christ in the world is called and empowered by the Holy Spirit to participate with God in God's mission of reconciliation, redemption, and liberation. Although having a unique and central role in God's plan of salvation, the church does not have exclusive rights on participation with God in God's mission. Thus many think it possible to cooperate with people of other faiths in God's universal mission. As the southern Indian theologian S. J. Samartha puts it, "In a religiously plural world, Christians, together with their neighbors of other faiths, are called upon to participate in God's continuing mission in the world. Mission is God's continuing activity through the Spirit to mend the brokenness of creation, to overcome the fragmentation of humanity, and to heal the rift between humanity, nature and God."[4]

The church's calling is to participate with God in mending the brokenness of creation and healing the rift between humanity, nature, and God. Echoing the biblical story, the mission of God, the mission of Jesus, and the mission of the church is one of reconciliation and redemption. This mission has a distinct bias toward those who are impoverished and marginalized, as Jesus was sent by God "to bring good news to the poor, . . . to proclaim release to the captives and recovery of sight to the blind, to let the oppressed go free, to proclaim the year of the Lord's favor" (Luke 4:18–19). God's mission, manifested in Jesus and empowered by the Holy Spirit, is not static but a centrifugal force of movement outward. Jesus demonstrated in word and deed that the reign of God, realized in the sending of God's Son, must continue to expand to the ends of the earth. "As you have sent me into the world, so I have sent them into the world" (John 17:18). Jesus's disciples are sent to bear his mission, God's mission, in the world.

For over a century and a half, the Episcopal Church has affirmed that baptism incorporates the faithful into the mission of God. The General Convention (the governing body of the Episcopal Church) proclaimed boldly in 1835 that the church was to be first and foremost a missionary society. All Episcopalians, by virtue of baptism and not voluntary association, were members of the Domestic and Foreign Missionary Society.[5] Participation in God's mission therefore is at the heart of the baptismal call. Baptism is thus a commission, co-mission, in God's mission. Just as God sent Jesus into the world, and Jesus sent his disciples to the ends of the earth, we too are sent in mission. The imperative is clear.

It is important to emphasize that the point of departure for participation in the *missio Dei* is baptism. Baptism, not ordination, is where the calling to a life of mission originates. The work of mission, the work of the church, belongs to the *laos,* as the people of God. Mission is not defined by activity or geographic location or holy orders but rather by the process of crossing frontiers from the known to the unknown, from the safe to the dangerous, from the comfortable to the uncomfortable.

Mission involves risk. It means risking oneself, one's control, and ultimately one's faith. Discovering God anew in those who are radically different and in unforeseen places is at the heart of mission. Moving beyond parochialism and provincialism in lives of worship, forgiveness, proclamation, service, and justice making, we are called to risk ourselves for the sake of God's reconciled creation. There is no more important work for each of us, individually and corporately, than to risk ourselves for the sake of God's mission.

What can one person do? One person can participate in the mission of God. If not us, as the followers of Christ, then who? If not now, then when? So . . . go . . . participate in God's mission of restoration and reconciliation!

2 ■ What Am I to Do When I Go?

The gospel imperatives—feed, clothe, heal, welcome, visit, raise, proclaim—are verbs of servant ministry. As baptized members of the Body of Christ, we are a missional community, chosen by God and helped by the Holy Spirit to bring justice to all people and creation. Through our baptism we become the Body of Christ, promising to take up Christ's mission. Indeed, as Presiding Bishop Michael Curry said, we are a people "living their Baptismal Covenant, following the teachings of Jesus, living the way of Jesus."[6] The Episcopal Church is the "Episcopal branch of the Jesus movement in the world."[7] Jesus started a movement and showed us the way of servanthood.

Read the Servant Song from Isaiah. Replace each "he" and "him" and insert your own name. As you read it imagine yourself as the servant of God who upholds you and whose Spirit rests on you.

> Here is my servant, whom I uphold,
>
> > my chosen, in whom my soul delights;
>
> I have put my spirit upon him;
>
> > he will bring forth justice to the nations.
>
> He will not cry or lift up his voice,
>
> > or make it heard in the street;
>
> a bruised reed he will not break,
>
> > and a dimly burning wick he will not quench;
>
> he will faithfully bring forth justice. (Isaiah 42:1–3)

How does that feel? What are you called to do as a servant of God?

Baptismal Promises

At baptism, candidates, or their parents and godparents, make five promises, called *baptismal promises*. These are promises to do the work God has given us to do in the world—our mission. Whenever we witness a baptism, confirmation, or reaffirmation, we renew our promises by answering the following questions with, "I will, with God's help":

> Will you continue in the apostles' teaching and fellowship, in the breaking of the bread, and in the prayers? *I will, with God's help.*
>
> Will you persevere in resisting evil, and whenever you fall into sin, repent, and return to the Lord? *I will, with God's help.*
>
> Will you proclaim by word and example the good news of God in Christ? *I will, with God's help.*
>
> Will you seek and serve Christ in all persons, loving your neighbor as yourself? *I will, with God's help.*
>
> Will you strive for justice and peace among all people, and respect the dignity of every human being? *I will, with God's help.*

Our promises begin with the community—the community of Christ's body, the Church—which nourishes us and encourages us to keep our baptismal promises. This first promise reminds us that we know ourselves first as members of a community of faith and that praying and receiving the sacraments prepares us for our work in the world. The second promise reminds us that before going out into the world we must make things right with ourselves—we must live according to God's will. We promise to resist evil and when we sin, to turn away and return to God.

The final three promises tell us about our mission in the world—how we are to serve others. We are to share the good news of God's love of all people both with our words and how we behave. That is, our actions are to reflect God's love. We are to seek and serve Christ in all people. That is, to look for the goodness in others and treat others as if they are Christ himself. As Matthew's gospel says in the parable of the goats and sheep, "Truly I tell you, just as you did it to one of the least of these who are members of my family, you did it to me" (25:40). We do this by feeding the hungry, clothing the poor, providing shelter for the homeless, and caring for the sick. In all that we do, we promise to strive for justice and peace among all people, that is, to deal fairly and honestly with others and work toward bringing all people together as one community. Because we are baptized Christians, living out these promises is our ministry and mission. When we are participating in God's mission, we are actively doing ministry.

Ministry in Daily Life

We carry out most of God's mission in our daily lives by greeting people kindly, doing our jobs with love and respect for others, lending a hand when needed, cooking for our family, and laughing and consoling friends and co-workers. We also carry out God's mission by working to change laws to ensure people are treated fairly. Occupations such as researching cures for disease, seeking to address climate change, lobbying government for just laws, and spending a year serving the poor either domestically or abroad are also ways of participating in God's mission. Through these actions we "carry out Christ's work of reconciliation in the world."

Let's look at reconciliation in the world more closely. What does reconciliation mean? Have you ever reconciled a bank statement? You compare your written record of deposits and withdrawals with the bank's records and make adjustments to your account until the two balances match. Think about the reconciliation of the world the same way. There are two things: the world as we actually live it and the world as God calls us to live (God's kingdom). So the work of reconciliation is making adjustments in how we live in an effort to make the world be a place of peace and wholeness.

So how do we live our ministry today? Many of us have loving families and friends, times when we laugh with others, basically healthy minds and bodies, and not too many roadblocks getting in the way of what we want. Some of us may face difficulties—loneliness, grief for the loss of a loved one, sickness and disease, discrimination and hatred, and perhaps days we don't have enough to eat or warm clothes to wear. The world falls short of what God would like. Although we may see signs of God's kingdom, it isn't here completely. To know what our ministry is, we need to understand what that kingdom looks like and figure out what we can do to help make it happen.

Jesus's Ministry Proclaiming the Kingdom of God

Jesus's words and actions show us God's dream for us by bringing joy, community, abundance, and justice to the world. One of the first things Jesus did after his baptism was to call together a community of people—his disciples. They worshiped, studied, and prayed together, and they saw Jesus performing miracles, healing, forgiving, and gathering more people together. Jesus also sent this group of ordinary people to continue to do God's work in the world.

The people Jesus called were ordinary people just like us. Some were fishermen; others did work that was despised in the Jewish community, like collecting taxes. The disciples weren't the smartest or the most faithful. Lots of times they doubted Jesus, and they fought over who was the most important. They weren't particularly reliable either. After all, they fell asleep in the garden the night before Jesus was crucified, even though he asked them to stay up with him. They had weaknesses just like we do. All this tells us that we too, even in our shortcomings, are part of God's beloved community called to carry out God's mission. If these seemingly unworthy followers of Jesus could help bring about God's kingdom, we can too. God does extraordinary things through ordinary people.

A Kingdom Marked by Justice

Soon after calling the first disciples, Jesus told them about the kingdom of God in the Sermon on the Mount, or the Beatitudes: blessed are those who mourn, blessed are the meek, blessed are those who hunger, blessed are the merciful, blessed are the pure in heart, blessed are the peacemakers, blessed are the persecuted and the reviled (Matthew 5). They are blessed because they will be comforted, inherit the earth, be filled, receive mercy, see God, and be called children of God. God's kingdom will be filled with justice.

A Kingdom Filled with Joy

Throughout Jesus's ministry he healed the sick and forgave those who had done wrong. Jesus brought them joy. What is amazing in these stories is how important touch was to his ministry of healing and forgiveness. For example, in Mark, Jesus touched a leper and said, "Be made clean," and the leper was cured. A woman who had been hemorrhaging for twelve years touched Jesus's cloak and was healed. Jesus laid his hands on the blind man to restore his sight. Touched by Jesus's healing power, these people could live out their lives with joy, free of disease. What we can learn from this is that while we might not be able to heal like Jesus, we can bring others joy by reaching out to them to let them know we care. And we can offer an embrace or handshake of forgiveness to those who have hurt us. By our touch we can bring joy to the world.

A Kingdom of Abundance

Jesus's ministry demonstrated what life is like when people are given more than they can ask or imagine. When the disciples were faced with a hungry crowd of more than five thousand people and only a few fish and a couple of loaves of bread, Jesus fed them all—with twelve baskets of food to spare. Nothing ran out. When people asked him to describe the kingdom of God, Jesus told about a mustard seed that grows into a tree that provides a home for the birds, yeast mixed with flour that expands into nourishing bread that can feed a village, and a field that yields a hundredfold. In Jesus's life of abundance, out of little comes much. We too can share what little we have, and together with others who have little, provide enough for everyone.

A Kingdom of a Community

Jesus was always calling a community together. He called the disciples, welcomed the outcast, and forgave the sinner. Consider the story of

Jesus and Zacchaeus, a Jewish tax collector, in Luke 19. Because Zacchaeus collected taxes for the Roman Empire, his own community considered him to be unclean and a sinner. He was an outcast. When Jesus came to him, he announced that they would dine together at Zacchaeus's house. So even before Zacchaeus confessed his sins, Jesus forgave him and invited him into his group of friends. Zacchaeus responded by repenting and giving back the taxes he'd stolen. Jesus gave Zacchaeus the strength to change his ways by forgiving him and bringing him back into the community. Jesus's acts of forgiveness restored community and brought peace. For Jesus, there's always more room at the table, and the community can always be expanded. In the parable of the Good Samaritan Jesus tells us that our neighbors are those who society says are unclean—those whom nobody seems to love. We, like Jesus, can invite others to our community—especially those who don't seem to belong.

We, Too, Are Called to Proclaim God's Dream

Jesus shared this ministry with his disciples, granting them the power and authority to heal and proclaim the kingdom of God. They continued this ministry after Jesus's death and resurrection, and with the power of the Holy Spirit they baptized believers to do the same. Through our baptism we too are part of the community that is sent out to do God's work. We too are called to a ministry of supporting relationships within community. We too are called to a ministry of abundance by providing for the needs of others. We too are called to a ministry of joy by healing the sick and comforting those who are mourning. We too are called to a ministry of justice by treating others fairly and honestly and asking others to do the same.

It's no mistake that our baptismal promises are all about living as God intends. We promise to seek and serve Christ in all persons, loving our neighbor as ourselves. And we promise to strive for justice and peace among all people and respect the dignity of every human being. We are called to do this, as Jesus did, from our community of faith. Through baptism we share in the mission and ministry of Jesus, a hands-on ministry marked by healing, forgiveness, blessing, and supporting others that proclaims that God's kingdom is near. We are members of the Jesus movement. Through our ministry we participate in God's kingdom of a life of joy, community, abundance, and justice.

3 ▪ How Am I Supported and Equipped to Go?

As a disciple of Jesus, in order to "go" out in our communities to live out the Gospel, we need tools and a support system. What if we viewed our faith community as a base camp? Hikers who do serious mountain climbing, like scaling Denali in Alaska or the Himalayas in Nepal, know how important a base camp is, how dependent they are on what it provides for their journey. Even nonhikers can imagine a list of what they find helpful and supportive:

- A staging area, launch pad, resting place, respite for restoring the spirit
- A safe haven, refuge from the storm, warmth, hospitality
- Encouragement, affirmation, celebration
- A nurturing environment for coming, going, returning
- Regrouping, retooling, restoring, refueling, renewing, rejuvenation
- Provisions: equipment, tools, repairs, food, and other supplies
- Training and acclimatization
- Healing when injured, emergency care
- Maps, guidance as to what is ahead
- Communications center, a place to share stories, connection with other base camps
- Community, fellowship

Impressive: A base camp can mean the difference between making an ascent and having to give up, between celebration and failure, between life and death.

Now take another look at that list. What would you strike as not being applicable for a Christian? The vast majority of this list reflects what any faith community would like to see as its reason for being: equipping individuals to live out their faith in the world.

From a Christian perspective, then, let us look at the base camp as a metaphor for the local congregation. Presbyterian pastor Steve Jacobsen put it this way:

> One image that may be useful is that of the church as a base camp. . . . The church is a base camp in which a community of people gathers to reflect on life, be reminded of their identity, and make plans for exploration. From there, each person goes out during the week to take on that part of the mountain that is theirs to explore. The base camp exists to serve the climbing team. In itself, it is neither the goal of the expedition nor the mountain itself. The value of this image is that it affirms the importance of the community . . . but does not mistake the institution for the central reality. The hikers don't exist for the good of the base camp. The base camp exists for the good of the hikers. The implications of this view of the church's role for working people are clear. The church needs to focus on its timeless tasks: it is to be a place of worship, education and community. But it also needs to evaluate how well it is empowering people for the work on the mountain those other six days. The church exists for the people, not the reverse. People deserve our help in making sense of all seven days.[8]

Let's be clear about what Jacobsen is saying, and what the base camp metaphor (as congregation) teaches us: The hikers (members) don't exist for the good of the base camp (faith community). The base camp exists for the good of the hikers.

What if we attended church to help us in living into our baptism in all the aspects of daily life? The concept of the congregation as base camp then calls us to move beyond concerns for a congregation's survival and programming, to see its role as "equipping the saints for the work of ministry" (Ephesians 4:12) in our day-to-day hiking/baptismal journeys. The Christian life is not unlike the hiker's journey with its straight and crooked places, its peaks and valleys, its potholes and smooth places. And every hiker needs the support of a base camp in order to engage in the journey.

When we understand the congregation as our base camp, the congregation is not therefore the destination, but a way station, staging area, watering hole, launch pad for the journey. The base camp (congregation) is a safe place and shelter—a place of refuge, renewal, regrouping, recommitment, restoring, refueling, retooling, refreshment, re-creation, and respite for reviving the spirit. It is a place of healing, emergency care, and repair; it is integral to the hikers' world, providing a bridge from liturgy to life. The base camp exists for the hikers. Their journeys are taken seriously. Worship becomes sustenance for the hard work of the climb. The Word is food for the spirit. The Bread and Wine are food for the journey.

The hike is wherever you spend time living life—work, family, community, school, leisure, and wider world. That is why the hike matters to God. Those are the venues where hikers spends their God-given gifts of time, talent, and ability. As in the Eucharist, Christ is really present in those places. "The Word became flesh and dwelt among us." It is the base camp's (congregation's) mission to guide, support, and equip you, the hiker, to live into that presence.

As with all metaphors, so with the base camp: It has its limitations. Unlike the Denali base camps, those working in the congregational base camp include not only those hired, but also many of the "hikers" who volunteer for liturgical, formation, and pastoral care ministries. But the focus of the metaphor is not lost. The vision is still on how those "in house" ministries are equipping the hikers for their callings in their daily lives. It also includes those who "come" to church.

The Lord is my *Sherpa*; I shall not want.

The Hiker's Commissioning

One expression of the hiker's commissioning is embedded in the Episcopal Church's catechism.[9]

> Q. Who are the ministers of the Church?
> A. The ministers of the Church are lay persons, bishops, priests, and deacons.
> Q. What is the ministry of the laity?
> A. The ministry of lay persons is to represent Christ and his Church; to bear witness to him wherever they may be; and, according to the gifts given them, to carry on Christ's work of reconciliation in the world; and to take their place in the life, worship, and governance of the Church.

The Book of Common Prayer lists laypersons as the first mentioned ministers: before bishops, before priests, before deacons. Notice too that the priorities of their ministry are "worldly," and that the "churchy" functions are left for last: "to take their place in the life, worship, and governance of the Church." Preceding that are the crucial ways that you are to live out your faith in the world—your hikes: "To represent Christ and his Church; to bear witness to him wherever they may be; and, according to the gifts given them, to carry on Christ's work of reconciliation in the world." The very insightful layperson Verna Dozier put it this way:

> Laypeople carry out those functions in the church (e.g., assist in the liturgy, serve on the vestry, teach church school, etc.), but to me they are always secondary functions for laity. The layperson's primary function is out there in the world.[10]

Jean Haldane, another layperson, reflected, "Let us see the laity as people who must be nurtured for ministry in society rather than as recruits for tasks in and for the church."[11] The key question then for us is to view our congregation as a Christian's base camp and how it is preparing, equipping, enhancing, affirming, and supporting you, its hiker, in your journey, in your primary ministry in the world to which you have been commissioned by your baptism—work, leisure, family, school, community, and wider world. It is for this ministerial/ missional priority in the world that the base camp exists. You may call for a paradigm shift in your view of what happens when you engage with your congregation.

The Hiker's Job Description

The Book of Common Prayer uses the Baptismal Covenant (pp. 304–5) as its primary job description for hikers with parallels in other denominations, such as the Evangelical Lutheran Church in America's *Evangelical Lutheran Worship* (pp. 232–44). The orientation of the Covenant is significant. First comes the Baptismal (Apostles') Creed. This foundational declaration roots each baptized person in an historic statement of faith. This sets the tone for why we, as Christians, live as we do. We are not humanists or atheists, promising to act for the greater good of society. We are first and foremost Christians, living out our lives rooted and grounded in the context of our faith in the Triune God: Father, Son, and Holy Spirit. It is that faith, which undergirds all that comes after, the raison d'être, the motivation for all that follows in the Covenant. We carry out the rest because of our belief in God: Father, Son, Holy Spirit. In the context of the Episcopal liturgy the entire congregation, in making this ancient baptismal statement of faith, joins the person being baptized, supported and accompanied by sponsors.

Celebrant Do you believe in God the Father?

People I believe in God, the Father almighty,
creator of heaven and earth.

Celebrant Do you believe in Jesus Christ, the Son of God?

People I believe in Jesus Christ, his only Son, our Lord.
He was conceived by the power of the Holy Spirit
and born of the Virgin Mary.
He suffered under Pontius Pilate,
was crucified, died, and was buried.
He descended to the dead.
On the third day he rose again.
He ascended into heaven,

> and is seated at the right hand of the Father.
> He will come again to judge the living and the dead.

Celebrant Do you believe in God the Holy Spirit?

People I believe in the Holy Spirit,
> the holy catholic Church,
> the communion of saints,
> the forgiveness of sins,
> the resurrection of the body,
> and the life everlasting.

Then, like concentric circles radiating out from the center, the Covenant moves from the base camp to the world.[12]

Celebrant Will you continue in the apostles' teaching
> and fellowship, in the breaking of bread, and
> in the prayers?

People I will, with God's help.

Celebrant Will you persevere in resisting evil, and,
> whenever you fall into sin, repent and return
> to the Lord?

People I will, with God's help.

These first two questions spell out the essential role of the base camp in the life of the hikers. For the hikers, life in that community is crucial for their journey—their ministry in daily life. The hikers depend on the congregation for their worship and nurture. "No man is an island," John Donne said. No Christian can be a Christian alone, apart from the body of Christ.

A county attorney who is a member of St. Paul's Episcopal Church in Richmond, Virginia, reflected:

> On Sundays, just being in the presence of each of you sharing the sacraments is both calming and renewing. The sense of community . . . uplifts me and supports me for the sometimes ugly conflict inherent in the political world. Our collective church community gives each of us the grace to stretch ourselves at work to be more fully in touch with spiritual values. I am motivated by the example set by other parishioners whose work proclaims Christ every day.[13]

For radical sending, investigate how your congregation provides support for its hikers (you) as you journey beyond the church doors by means of worship, formation, pastoral care, and communications:

- How does teaching, fellowship, and prayers prepare you for your primary ministry in your world of daily living?
- How is its Eucharist truly "food for the journey"?
- How does its worship both nurture and challenge you?
- How is your faith community a resource for reconciliation when you fall short in daily life?

It is one thing to profess our faith standing among other Christians in a church building on a Sunday. It is totally different to live into that faith the other six days of the week in those other buildings we inhabit. That is why what happens on Sunday is so important. It is there in the congregation that the disciples are equipped for the challenges encountered during those other six days.

The Covenant continues with a shift to the life of the hikers outside

28

the congregation—in their world of home, job, school, leisure, community, and wider world.[14]

Celebrant	Will you proclaim by word and example the Good News of God in Christ?
People	I will, with God's help.
Celebrant	Will you seek and serve Christ in all persons, loving your neighbor as yourself?
People	I will, with God's help.
Celebrant	Will you strive for justice and peace among all people, and respect the dignity of every human being?
People	I will, with God's help.

A manager of a county community corrections program, also a member of St. Paul's Episcopal Church in Richmond, reflected:

> One statement from the Baptismal Covenant has had special emphasis for me: "I will respect the dignity of every human being." It is a core value.... To be effective in working with mandated clients, people from all walks of life, it helps to look for the human potential, each person's strengths and who they are, not just their problems or what they have done.[15]

Verna Dozier states it clearly:

> If I believe that there is a loving God, who has created me and wants me to be part of a people who will carry the good news of the love of that God to the world, what

difference does that make when I go to my office at nine o'clock Monday morning? What difference does it make in my office that I believe there is a loving God, that God loves me, and that God loves all human beings exactly as that God loves me? What different kinds of decisions do I make? What am I called to do in that office?[16]

This is the essence of discipleship. This is where the rubber meets the road, where the action is—in the daily life of the baptized where they meet and celebrate and struggle, where all the nurturing and preparation pays off in ministry. In boardrooms and bedrooms, on firing lines and assembly lines, among legislators and landscapers, in courts of law and on tennis courts, in kitchens and kindergartens, in repair shops and coffee shops, among artists and architects, in hospitals and hotels—wherever the laos, the people of God are living and working and playing. Quite a ministry! And in that world of daily life, the laity carry out the functions of bishop, priest, and deacon. The teacher *oversees* a classroom day-by-day (the bishop's function). The parent and the office worker on occasion *bless* and *affirm*, *forgive* and *reconcile* (a priest's function). And, at their best, the waiter or the manager provides *servant* leadership (the deacon's function). The ordained carry out these functions in the ordered life of the church; the laity carry them out in their daily lives.

What a calling, what a vocation, what a ministry! Those empowering words belong to all the people of God. From the commissioning to the job description, and now to our marching orders: the radical sending, the Dismissal.

The Hikers' Marching Orders

Jesus was quite clear with his followers: "You are the salt of the earth. . . . You are the light of the world" (Matthew 5:13–14). As followers of Jesus, we are not free to exist for our own selves—we are sent out to have an impact on our surroundings—like salt and light. We are to transform our environment.

St. Teresa of Ávila, a sixteenth-century Spanish mystic, wrote:

> Christ has no body now on earth but yours; no hands but yours, no feet but yours. Yours are the eyes through which the compassion of Christ must look out on the world. Yours are the feet with which He is to go about doing good. Yours are the hands with which He is to bless His people.

Teresa understands "clothing ourselves with Christ" to be a matter of becoming *alter Christi*, "other Christs," in the world, so that the faithful serve as Christ's very eyes and ears and presence among the people. Hence, at the end of the Episcopal liturgy, come our marching orders:

> And now Father, send us out to do the work you have given us to do, to love and serve you as faithful witnesses of Christ our Lord. . . . Let us go forth into the world, rejoicing in the power of the Spirit.[17]

The liturgy is clear that the work of Christian living is not limited to the worship experience; instead, we are commissioned to use the provisioning that worship provides to sustain us in our true calling, our work "out there" in the world. Our challenge, then, is to engage

31

in liturgy as the life-giving enterprise it is intended to be, so that we might not only "become what we receive,"[18] as John H. McKenna expresses it, but also that we might share with the world at large, in our daily lives, all that God has so bountifully provided. When the words and actions are truly life-giving, their power cannot be contained inside the building. When the liturgy comes to life, the liturgy becomes connected to life. When the liturgy becomes life-giving, it connects with real life.

Consequently, the sending or Dismissal after the worship is most compelling when it is the culmination of all that has gone before it—praise, prayer, exhortation, communion, homily, and testimony. How we use worship to feed and sustain the faithful is important. But how we (the faithful) are sent out to do the work God has given us to do is the hallmark of transformational worship. Our time inside the church building bears fruit when we carry the message into our Monday-through-Sunday lives. If we get the Dismissal right, we get everything right, and "make the whole world Eucharist."[19]

Dr. Seuss, an unexpected resource for Christian doctrine, put it this way in *Oh, the Places You'll Go!*:

> You're off to Great Places!
>
> Today is your day!
>
> Your mountain is waiting.
>
> So . . . get on your way![20]

As Christ ascended, the "men in white" in Acts 1 asked the disciples, "Why do you stand looking up toward heaven?" We're sent out into the world for a reason. As a preacher has put it, "Jesus has left the building—and we will find him out there on the streets." Lutherans refer to the concluding hymn as the "Sending Song."

Along with receiving food for our journey, the most important thing about going to church on Sunday is leaving. After all, God has much for us to do and we need to be about it. Go!

Thanks be to God!

4 ▪ What Are My Gifts for Mission and Ministry?

In letters to early Christian communities in Corinth, Galatia, and Rome, the apostle Paul wrote about gifts of the Spirit: talents and abilities God gives us to fulfill our mission in the world. Paul was addressing the struggles these communities were facing. What were their ministries? What gifts did the people have to fulfill their mission? How could the individuals in the community work together as one? We continue to ask ourselves these very same questions. This is what we learn from Paul.

There are a variety of gifts. In 1 Corinthians 12:4–10, Paul lists the following gifts: wisdom, knowledge, faith, healing, working of miracles, prophecy, discernment of spirits, tongues, and the interpretation of tongues. And in Paul's letter to the Romans he lists more gifts: ministry, teaching, exhortation, generosity, diligence, and cheerfulness (Romans 12:6–8). Both lists addressed the needs of the communities to whom Paul had written; neither was meant to be exhaustive. The Spirit gives different gifts at different times to meet the changing needs of the community.

Every member of the Body of Christ has been given spiritual gifts to take their place in God's mission, and each person's gift is different from everyone else's. Remember, community is important to God. While everyone has at least one gift, no one has them all. No one is meant to pursue God's mission alone. The Body of Christ has many members, and the gifts of each are to be used in partnership with others. In 1 Corinthians 12, Paul talks about the Church as a human body. The body has many parts, each necessary to the health of the body but none sufficient on its own. "If the foot would say, 'Because I am not a hand, I do not belong to the body,' that would not make it any less a part of the body." And also, "The eye cannot say to the hand, 'I have no need of you'" (1 Corinthians 12:15, 21). Suppose the person with vision didn't share her gift? Imagine the harm a body could do if it couldn't see what it was doing. You need to use your gifts along with the gifts of others to serve God's kingdom.

God provides spiritual gifts generously. Hidden behind what might not seem like much is something beyond imagination. You, together with others in your community, have all the gifts you need to do to bring about God's kingdom. In fact, God gives even more than we need. Read the parable of the sower in Mark's gospel (4:3–9). The farmer threw seeds all over the place: on the path, on rocky ground, among thorns, and on good soil. God is like that—giving generously and hoping that the seeds will take root. Our job is to receive God's gifts and nurture them to bear fruit.

Use Your Gifts for the Good of Everyone

Superheroes in the movies can show us what's possible with abundant gifts. Superman flies with lightning speed to save a person in need. Wonder Woman lifts meteors the size of small cities. Batman has supersized powers to fight evil and crime in Gotham City. That's what abundant gifts look like—enough to fight oppression, avert disasters, challenge violence, and renew life. Take a minute and imagine what you could do if your gifts were supersized. If you had unlimited generosity or wisdom, what would you do differently?

We are to use our gifts not to boost ourselves, but to serve others.

The apostle Paul tells us the same thing. Each member uses their gifts for the good of the family, bringing the community to its greatest ability to live into their call. You may not be a superhero fit for the big screen, but when you use your gifts in everyday acts of ministry, you're an everyday hero. What may seem like simple acts to you can be great acts of ministry to others.

God created you and blessed you and wants you, and all of God's people, to have joy. So using your gifts will also energize you and make you feel good. Paul talked about joy in terms of the fruit of the Spirit. In his letter to the Galatians (5:22–23) he lists the following fruit: love, joy, peace, patience, kindness, generosity, faithfulness, gentleness, and self-control. The qualities suggest a life of joy in relationship with others.

We are adept at doing many things. Modern life seems to require this. In your daily life, when managing your household and fulfilling your work and community obligations, you may be required to write reports, lead meetings, plan events, diagnose diseases, operate heavy machinery, and so on. You are likely good at many things. But just because you might be good at something doesn't mean it is your gift. What makes a skill a gift is that you look forward to using gifts; using your skills tends to deplete your energy. This doesn't mean you cannot or should not use your skills; it is just a way to look for those things that come from your heart—your gifts.

You can use your gifts for lots of purposes. You can use them to bring people together or use them selfishly for your own gain; you can use them to build relationships or to tear them down; to nourish life or to destroy it. What we learn from the Bible and the Christian community is that God has given you gifts to build community,

37

strengthen relationships, nourish and support life, and bring people closer to God. As Christians we recognize that our gifts originate with God and we must use them for God's mission, the kingdom of God, and not for our own purposes.

As noted, each of us has gifts for ministry. And each of us has the responsibility to find out what those gifts are. Once we come to know those gifts we can nurture and honor them by offering them to God and practicing them in our ministry to proclaim the kingdom of God.

The process that helps us come to know our gifts is called *discernment*, which pulls apart the various possibilities to allow us to see each more clearly. It is a process of distinguishing the variety of gifts— our gifts from those of others and those of the Spirit from gifts not of the Spirit. The work of discernment is never finished. Our gifts change, the needs of the community change, and consequently our call will change. You can ask yourself two very broad questions to help you in discerning your gifts: (1) What do I long to do? And (2) How do the things I long to do fit into God's mission?

As Parker Palmer states, "Before you tell your life what you intend to do with it, listen to what it intends to do with you."[21] God has called us to go forth in ministry. God does not leave us to our own devices; God gives us gifts for the work we have been given to do, "to love and serve you [God] as faithful witnesses of Christ our Lord."[22]

5 ▪ Why Does This Matter?

Jesus told this story to explain the importance of our actions:

> There was a rich man who was dressed in purple and fine linen and who feasted sumptuously every day. And at his gate lay a poor man named Lazarus, covered with sores, who longed to satisfy his hunger with what fell from the rich man's table; even the dogs would come and lick his sores.
>
> The poor man died and was carried away by the angels to be with Abraham. The rich man also died and was buried. In Hades, where he was being tormented, he looked up and saw Abraham far away with Lazarus by his side. He called out, "Father Abraham, have mercy on me, and send Lazarus to dip the tip of his finger in water and cool my tongue; for I am in agony in these flames." But Abraham said, "Child, remember that during your lifetime you received your good things, and Lazarus in like manner evil things; but now he is comforted here, and you are in agony. Besides all this, between you and us a great chasm has been fixed, so that those who might want to pass from here to you cannot do so, and no one can cross from there to us."
>
> He said, "Then, father, I beg you to send him to my father's house—for I have five brothers—that he may warn them, so that they will not also come into this place of torment." Abraham replied, "They have Moses and the prophets; they should listen to them." He said, "No, father Abraham; but if someone goes to them from the dead, they

will repent." He said to him, "If they do not listen to Moses and the prophets, neither will they be convinced even if someone rises from the dead." (Luke 16:19–31)

There is a man at the gate and it matters how we treat him. It matters to the man, it matters to Jesus, and most of all it matters to God. It matters how the wealthy man treats Lazarus specifically and how the rich treat the poor generally. Day after day, as he passed through the gates, the rich man paid no attention to Lazarus. God, on the other hand, has a special concern for the man at the gate.

Jesus makes it clear that, if we love him, he expects us to care for those who have been abandoned, marginalized—for the sheep who have no shepherd. Remember the questions the resurrected Christ asked Simon Peter:

> "Simon, son of John, do you love me more than these?"
> . . . Peter felt hurt because he said to him the third time,
> "Do you love me?" And he said to him, "Lord, you know
> everything; you know that I love you." Jesus said to him,
> "Feed my sheep." (John 21:15, 17)

True, we are responsible for ourselves. But what the parable and the passage teach, which is radical, is that we are also responsible for the people in our lives and in the world around us. That is a hard message to hear. I am responsible for myself, and, to a lesser extent, I am responsible for my family. I have responsibilities at work; I can reach out and help people. But does God really expect me to be responsible for the man at the gate? Why? And how? This work is more than just the rich tending the poor, though that is certainly part of it. Caring is often seen as something the "haves" do for the "have nots." But Jesus's challenge to us all is one that goes far beyond *noblesse oblige*, the condescending acts of the nobility on behalf of the poor. The radical message here is that we care for each other, I for you and you for me. This moves us beyond the notion of a Samaritan helping out a beaten and abandoned neighbor or a rich man helping out a poor man. On the contrary, Jesus's message is that we are now part of a radically reconfigured family wherein each one is a brother and sister for whom we are responsible.

Through the cross, Jesus has taken on responsibility for us, for the whole world. Now he needs us to do the same, to take up our cross and follow, and care for the world in which we live. That makes us responsible for our communities, our cities, our states, our nation, other nations, even our enemies. All the sheep are our responsibility.

Not just the ones who are like us.

Not just the ones who go to our church.

Not just the other Episcopalians.

Not just the Christians.

The hard lesson here, one we are all too eager as sinful broken human beings to ignore, is that it matters to God how we live and how we care for and stand with others. There is someone standing at the gate of our lives. And that person, that community, is waiting for us to stand with them as extensions of God's mercy, grace, and abundant love.

Luke is thoughtful enough to realize this message can sound harsh and demanding; thankfully, he also sends a message of hope. Luke believes that once you choose to follow Jesus, the power of the Holy Spirit sweeps in and incredible things are suddenly possible. You can take up your cross. You can tend and feed neighbors near and far. Luke knows we can reflect the goodness and grace of the God who made and redeemed us. Because of the Spirit's power pulsing at the heart of Christian community, we can take up our responsibility for one another, and share our lives for the glory of God.

Good and Dangerous News

In the Acts of Apostles, Luke provides yet another story of Christians who act out of deep care and solidarity with the suffering.

This time, the disciples Peter and John were on their way into the temple and saw a man at the gate. Every day his friends brought him to the gate of the temple, called the Beautiful Gate, hoping he would be cured, healed, or at least receive some measure of kindness.

The man at the gate reached out to Peter and John. Peter told him, "I have no silver or gold, but what I have I give you; in the name of Jesus Christ of Nazareth, stand up and walk." Then Peter takes his hand, raises him up, and sends him leaping and praising God on his way into the temple (Acts 3:1–8).

You and I offer a unique witness to God's plan for the salvation of the world through Jesus Christ. There is no theme, no hopeful message, no political agenda more transformative than the good news of salvation in Jesus Christ. We as Christians know a source of real healing for a hurting world; we have access to transformation for people in dire physical and spiritual need.

We are not in the business of persuading others of the truth of the gospel story through propositional argument. As Anglican theologian John Milbank claims, we are not about conversion through arguing about beliefs, which often becomes an act of violence against others.[23]

Andy Doyle, Bishop of Texas, says we are "about the work of 'out-narrating' the world around us. By this, I simply mean there are rival narratives about what the world is, who God is, whether God is. We need to claim our unique proclamation of the greatest story there is to tell."[24]

We as Christians can live out our faith so that others are attracted by the sublime beauty of God reflected in the church at work in the world. We, the church, are called to be what theologian Stanley Hauerwas calls a "community of character," embodying a "peaceable kingdom."[25] We are called to exhibit in our corporate life the radical alternative life of those who follow Christ. At baptism, we are marked with this sacred story on our foreheads, and thus marked as Christ's own forever. Hands are laid upon us by a bishop at confirmation and sometimes at reception into the Episcopal Church to empower us by the same Holy Spirit for a life of discovery, formation, and mission.

Like Peter and John, we have received the sacred story of transformation, of sin and redemption, death and resurrection, sickness and healing. Each one of the saints that has come before us has passed the narrative to us. Over the centuries the proclamation of this good news of salvation has out-narrated the secular world's story of hopelessness. Thousands of Christian saints, from Saint Peter Abelard with his poetry to Saint Francis with his actions, have proclaimed and given voice to the story, "that after his resurrection Jesus ascended into heaven and at the end of the age he will come in glory to judge the living and the dead and to finally and fully manifest the kingly rule of God over all of creation."[26]

As Episcopalians we go further, making a unique proclamation of the Christian faith. Several themes are at the heart of this uniquely

Episcopal proclamation of the good news. They are captured in our Baptismal Covenant. They guide our living of the gospel message:

1. Our Episcopal faith is supported by our continued reflection on Scripture, the apostles' teachings, communal prayer, and life lived in connection with the sacraments.

2. Mission is the work of God, who was sent into the world and sends us into the world. When we enact the gospel, we make Jesus Christ incarnate in the world. Mission and outreach are about Jesus: first, last, and always.

3. Mission and outreach are holistic. We seek to meet the needs of the whole person, spiritual and physical.

4. We proclaim in voice and in action the good news of the reign of God.

5. We teach, baptize, and nurture believers.

6. We respond to human need by serving others.

7. We transform unjust structures of society.

8. We seek sustainable and renewing initiatives that redeem not only humanity but the creation in which we live.

9. Our outreach and mission are always rooted in Scripture, tradition, and reason.

10. We make a greater witness to the world around us when we join hands with one another beyond differences of theology, ideology, and identity, in order to meet the human needs around us.

11. We are changed by serving and walking with others. We are incomplete without the poor, voiceless, and oppressed by our side.

12. We are saved and given power to serve and act only by God's grace.

This is the unique story of our faith. It is the particular story which gives meaning to the chaos of a world ruled by powers and principalities. It is what we have been given by Jesus of Nazareth and what we have to offer the world.

How we believe, how we communicate about God and the story we have received, is a prism, a scope, through which the entire world around us makes the most sense. That is what Episcopal means: *Epi* means "on or above," and *scope* means "to see in order to act, to target, to observe." Our unique Episcopal version of the gospel understands that we see and act for the whole world—including the man at the gate.

Sharing a Mission and a Message

Because of our common mission, we are uniquely prepared to be God's people in the world. Now we are responsible for sharing it: the mission and the message. There are people outside our doors, and every congregation and person in the Episcopal Church bears a responsibility that leads us unashamedly, unabashedly into the world to meet them. You may not have gold or silver, but you have what you have received: grace and mercy.

Our baptism calls us to action. It calls us to proclaim by word and example the Good News of God in Christ. It calls us to seek and serve Christ in all persons, loving our neighbors as ourselves. It calls us to strive for justice and peace among all people, respecting the dignity of every human being. It is not easy and not always comfortable. But we do all this with God's help and the faith community that feeds us in word, sacrament, and fellowship.

> Eternal God, heavenly Father,
>
> you have graciously accepted us as living members
>
> of your Son our Savior Jesus Christ,
>
> and you have fed us with spiritual food
>
> in the Sacrament of his Body and Blood.
>
> Send us now into the world in peace,
>
> and grant us strength and courage
>
> to love and serve you
>
> with gladness and singleness of heart;
>
> through Jesus Christ our Lord. Amen.[27]

Notes

1 See Johannes Blauw, *The Missionary Nature of the Church* (New York: McGraw-Hill, 1962), and Donald Senior and Carroll Stuhlmueller, *The Biblical Foundations for Mission* (Maryknoll, NY: Orbis Books, 1984).

2 Book of Common Prayer, 855.

3 David J. Bosch, *Transforming Mission: Paradigm Shifts in Theology of Mission* (Maryknoll, NY: Orbis Books, 1991), 392.

4 S. J. Samartha, *One Christ—Many Religions: Towards a Revised Christology* (Maryknoll, NY: Orbis Books, 1995), 149.

5 *Journal of the Proceedings of the Bishops, Clergy and Laity of the Protestant Episcopal Church in the United States of America in a General Convention 1835* (New York: Swords, Stanford and Company, 1935), 130–31.

6 Michael Curry, *Crazy Christians: A Call to Follow Jesus* (Harrisburg, PA: Morehouse, 2013), 101.

7 Michael Curry, "First address as Presiding Bishop," Episcopal Church, https://www.episcopalchurch.org/post/publicaffairs/presiding-bishop-michael-curry-jesus-movement-and-we-are-episcopal.church.

8 Steve Jacobsen, *Hearts to God, Hands to Work* (Herndon, VA: Alban Institute, 1997), 24.

9 Book of Common Prayer, 855.

10 Verna Dozier, *The Authority of the Laity* (Washington, DC: Alban Institute, 1984), 40.

11 Jean M. Haldane, "Ministry of Laity in Daily Life," *Action Information*, Washington, DC, Alban Institute, July/August 1989, https://oca.org/parish-ministry/theology/ministry-of-laity-in-daily-life (accessed August 13, 2018).

12 Book of Common Prayer, 304.

13 A Faith@Work article in the St. Paul's, Richmond, Virginia, monthly Epistle, September 2007.

14 Book of Common Prayer, 305.

15 St. Paul's, Richmond Virginia, monthly Epistle, June 2005.

16 Dozier, *Authority of the Laity*, 16.

17 Book of Common Prayer, 366.

18 John H. McKenna, *Become What We Receive: A Systematic Study of the Eucharist* (Chicago/Mundelein, IL: Hillenbrand Books, 2012), and quote by the Reverend Margaret Bullitt-Jonas in a sermon preached on August 3, 2008, http://revivingcreation.org/behold-what-you-are-become-what-you-receive/ (accessed August 13, 2018).

19 Teillard de Chardin, *Hymn of the Universe* (San Francisco: HarperCollins, 1974).

20 Dr. Seuss, *Oh, the Places You'll Go!* (New York: Random House, 1990), 56.

21 Parker J. Palmer, *Let Your Life Speak* (San Francisco: Jossey-Bass, 2000), 3.

22 Book of Common Prayer, 366.

23 Quoted in "Sharing the Gospel of Salvation: GS Misc 956" (London: General Synod of the Church of England, 2010), sec. 72.

24 C. Andrew Doyle, *Unabashedly Episcopalian: Proclaiming the Good News of the Episcopal Church* (New York: Morehouse, 2012), 86.

25 "Sharing the Gospel of Salvation," sec. 73.

26 "Sharing the Gospel of Salvation," sec. 11.

27 Book of Common Prayer, 365.

Resources for Further Exploration

For digging deeper into baptismal ministry:

Cottrell, Stephen, Steven Croft, Paula Gooder, Robert Atwell, and Sharon Ely Pearson. *Pilgrim: Church & Kingdom, A Course for the Christian Journey.* New York: Church Publishing, 2016.

Curry, Michael B., and others. *Following the Way of Jesus.* Vol. 6. Church's Teachings for a Changing World. New York: Church Publishing, 2017.

Doyle, C. Andrew. *Unabashedly Episcopalian: Proclaiming the Good News of the Episcopal Church.* New York: Morehouse, 2012.

Palmer, Parker J. *Let Your Life Speak: Listening to the Voice of Vocation.* San Francisco: Jossey-Bass, 2000.

Prentiss, Demi, and Fletcher Lowe. *Radical Sending: Go to Love and Serve.* New York: Morehouse, 2015.

Varghese, Winne. *Church Meets World.* Vol. 4. Church's Teachings for a Changing World. New York: Church Publishing, 2016.

Westerhoff, John H. *Living Faithfully as a Prayer Book People.* Harrisburg, PA: Morehouse, 2004.

For examples of living out baptismal ministry:

Adams, Mark, Minerva Carcaño, Gerald Kicanas, Kirk Smith, and Stephen Talmage. *Bishops of the Border: Pastoral Responses to Immigration.* Harrisburg, PA: Morehouse, 2013.

Alkire, Sabrina, and Edmund Newell. *What Can One Person Do? Faith to Heal a Broken World.* New York: Church Publishing, 2005.

Heaney, Robert S., Zeyneb Sayilgan, and Claire Haymes, eds. *Faithful Neighbors: Christian-Muslim Vision and Practice.* New York: Morehouse, 2016.

Lloyd, Lallie B. *All Our Children: The Church's Call to Address Education Inequity.* New York: Church Publishing, 2017.

Meeks, Catherine, ed. *Living into God's Dream: Dismantling Racism in America.* New York: Morehouse, 2016.

Wells, Samuel. *How Then Shall We Live? Christian Engagement with Contemporary Issues.* New York: Church Publishing, 2017.

TURN: Pause, listen, and choose to follow Jesus

THE WAY OF LOVE

As Jesus was walking along, he saw Levi son of Alphaeus sitting at the tax booth, and he said to him, "Follow me." And he got up and followed him.
– Mark 2:14

"Do you turn to Jesus Christ . . . ?"
– Book of Common Prayer, 302

Like the disciples, we are called by Jesus to follow the Way of Love. With God's help, we can turn from the powers of sin, hatred, fear, injustice, and oppression toward the way of truth, love, hope, justice, and freedom. In turning, we reorient our lives to Jesus Christ, falling in love again, again, and again.

For Reflection and Discernment

- What practices help you to turn again and again to Jesus and the Way of Love?
- How will (or do) you incorporate these practices into your rhythm of life?
- Who will be your companion as you turn toward Jesus?

LEARN: Reflect on Scripture each day, especially on Jesus's life and teachings.

"Those who love me will keep my word, and my Father will love them, and we will come to them and make our home with them." – John 14:23

Grant us so to hear [the Holy Scriptures], read, mark, learn, and inwardly digest them. – Book of Common Prayer, 236

By reading and reflecting on Scripture, especially the life and teachings of Jesus, we draw near to God, and God's word dwells in us. When we open our minds and hearts to Scripture, we learn to see God's story and God's activity in everyday life.

For Reflection and Discernment

- What ways of reflecting on Scripture are most life-giving for you?
- When will you set aside time to read and reflect on Scripture in your day?
- With whom will you share in the commitment to read and reflect on Scripture?

PRAY: Dwell intentionally with God daily

He was praying in a certain place, and after he had finished,
  one of his disciples said to him, "Lord, teach us to pray,
  as John taught his disciples." – Luke 11:1
"Lord, hear our prayer." – Book of Common Prayer

Jesus teaches us to come before God with humble hearts, boldly offering our thanksgivings and concerns to God or simply listening for God's voice in our lives and in the world. Whether in thought, word, or deed, individually or corporately, when we pray we invite and dwell in God's loving presence.

For Reflection and Discernment

- What intentional prayer practices center you in God's presence, so you can hear, speak, or simply dwell with God?
- How will (or do) you incorporate intentional prayer into your daily life?
- With whom will you share in the commitment to pray?

WORSHIP: Gather in community weekly to thank, praise, and dwell with God

When he was at the table with them, he took bread, blessed and broke it,
  and gave it to them. Then their eyes were opened, and they recognized him.
  – Luke 24:30-31

Celebrant: Lift up your hearts. People: We lift them to the Lord.
  – Book of Common Prayer, 361

When we worship, we gather with others before God. We hear the Good News of Jesus, give thanks, confess, and offer the brokenness of the world to God. As we break bread, our eyes are opened to the presence of Christ. By the power of the Holy Spirit, we are made one body, the body of Christ sent forth to live the Way of Love.

For Discernment and Reflection

- What communal worship practices move you to encounter God and knit you into the body of Christ?
- How will (or do) you commit to regularly worship?
- With whom will you share the commitment to worship this week?

BLESS: Share faith and unselfishly give and serve

"Freely you have received; freely give." – Matthew 10:8

Celebrant: Will you proclaim by word and example the Good News of God in Christ?
People: We will, with God's help. – Book of Common Prayer, 305

Jesus called his disciples to give, forgive, teach, and heal in his name. We are empowered by the Spirit to bless everyone we meet, practicing generosity and compassion and proclaiming the Good News of God in Christ with hopeful words and selfless actions. We can share our stories of blessing and invite others to the Way of Love.

For Discernment and Reflection

- What are the ways the Spirit is calling you to bless others?
- How will (or does) blessing others through sharing your resources, faith, and story become part of your daily life?
- Who will join you in committing to the practice of blessing others

GO: Cross boundaries, listen deeply, and live like Jesus

Jesus said to them, "Peace be with you. As the Father has sent me,
so I send you." – John 20:21

Send them into the world in witness to your love.
– Book of Common Prayer, 306

As Jesus went to the highways and byways, he sends us beyond our circles and comfort to witness to the love, justice, and truth of God with our lips and with our lives. We go to listen with humility and to join God in healing a hurting world. We go to become Beloved Community, a people reconciled in love with God and one another.

For Discernment and Reflection

- To what new places or communities is the Spirit sending you to witness to the love, justice, and truth of God?
- How will you build into your life a commitment to cross boundaries, listen carefully, and take part in healing and reconciling what is broken in this world?
- With whom will you share in the commitment to go forth as a reconciler and healer?

REST: Receive the gift of God's grace, peace, and restoration

Peace I leave with you; my peace I give you. I do not give to you
as the world gives. Do not let your hearts be troubled
and do not be afraid. – John 14:27

Blessed are you, O Lord . . . giving rest to the weary,
renewing the strength of those who are spent.
– Book of Common Prayer, 113

From the beginning of creation, god has established the sacred pattern of going and returning, labor and rest. Especially today, God invites us to dedicate time for restoration and wholeness—within our bodies, minds, and souls, and within our communities and institutions. By resting, we place our trust in God; the primary actor who brings all things to their fullness.

For Discernment and Reflection

- What practices restore your body, mind and soul?
- How will you observe rest and renewal on a regular basis?
- With whom will you commit to create and maintain a regular practice of rest?

9 781640 651784